OCEAN
FOOD WEBS

BY PAUL FLEISHER

LERNER PUBLICATIONS COMPANY • MINNEAPOLIS

The photographs in this book are used with the permission of: © John Foxx/Stockbyte/Getty Images, backgrounds on pp. 1, 6, 13, 20, 24, 31, 36, 45, 46, 47; Courtesy of Larry Benvenuti, National Oceanic and Atmospheric Administration Central Library Photo Collection, p. 5; Courtesy of NOAA, p. 6; © Reinhard Dirsherl/Visuals Unlimited, pp. 7, 33, 47; © PHONE Gohier François/Peter Arnold, Inc., p. 9; © David Wrobel/Visuals Unlimited, pp. 10, 13, 21, 25; © S. E. Arndt/Peter Arnold, Inc., p. 11; © Fritz Polking/Peter Arnold, Inc., p. 12; © Hal Beral/Visuals Unlimited, p. 15; © altrendo travel/Getty Images, p. 16; © Konrad Wothe/Look/Getty Images, p. 17; © Chuck Davis/Stone/Getty Images, p. 18; © Peter David/Taxi/Getty Images, p. 19; © Daniel W. Gotshall/Visuals Unlimited, p. 20; © Glenn Oliver/Visuals Unlimited, p. 22; © Brandon Cole Marine Photography/Alamy, p. 23; © John Seagrim/Taxi/Getty Images, p. 24; © Richard Herrmann/Visuals Unlimited, p. 26; © David McNew/Peter Arnold, Inc., p. 27; © Mike Anich/Visuals Unlimited, p. 28; © Marty Snyderman/Visuals Unlimited, p. 29; © Aldo Brando/Stone/Getty Images, p. 30; © Paul Nicklen/National Geographic/Getty Images, p. 31; © Paolo Curto/The Image Bank/Getty Images, p. 32; © SAS/Alamy, p. 34; © Michael Nichols/National Geographic/Getty Images, p. 35; © Wolfgang Poelzer/Peter Arnold, Inc., p. 36; © Stuart Paton/The Image Bank/Getty Images, p. 37; © DEA/M. BERTINELLI/De Agostini Picture Library/Getty Images, p. 38; © ullstein-Teich/Peter Arnold, Inc., p. 39; © BIOS Borrell Bartomeu/Peter Arnold, Inc., p. 40; © Leroy Simon/Visuals Unlimited, p. 41; © Ray Pfortner/Peter Arnold, Inc., p. 42; © Jeff Greenberg/Peter Arnold, Inc., p. 43; Courtesy of Mike White, NOAA's Coral Kingdom Collection, p. 46; Courtesy of the Florida Keys National Marine Sanctuary Staff, NOAA's Coral Kingdom Sanctuary; p. 48 (both). Illustrations on pp. 4, 14 by Zeke Smith, © Lerner Publishing Group, Inc.; map on p. 8 © Laura Westlund/Independent Picture Service.

Cover: © David Wrobel/Visuals Unlimited (top); © Richard Herrmann/Visuals Unlimited (bottom left); Courtesy of Florida Keys National Marine Sanctuary, part of the NOAA Central Library Photo Collection (bottom right); © John Foxx/Stockbyte/Getty Images (background).

Lerner Publications Company
A division of Lerner Publishing Group, Inc.
241 First Avenue North
Minneapolis, MN 55401 U.S.A.

Website address: www.lernerbooks.com

Library of Congress Cataloging-in-Publication Data

Fleisher, Paul.
    Ocean food webs / by Paul Fleisher.
        p.   cm. —   (Early bird food webs)
    ISBN 978–0–8225–6732–5 (lib. bdg. : alk. paper)
    1. Marine ecology—Juvenile literature. 2. Food chains (Ecology)—Juvenile literature. I. Title.
QH541.5.S3F54 2008
577.7—dc22   2006035853

Manufactured in the United States of America
1 2 3 4 5 6 – JR – 13 12 11 10 09 08

CONTENTS

An Ocean Food Web

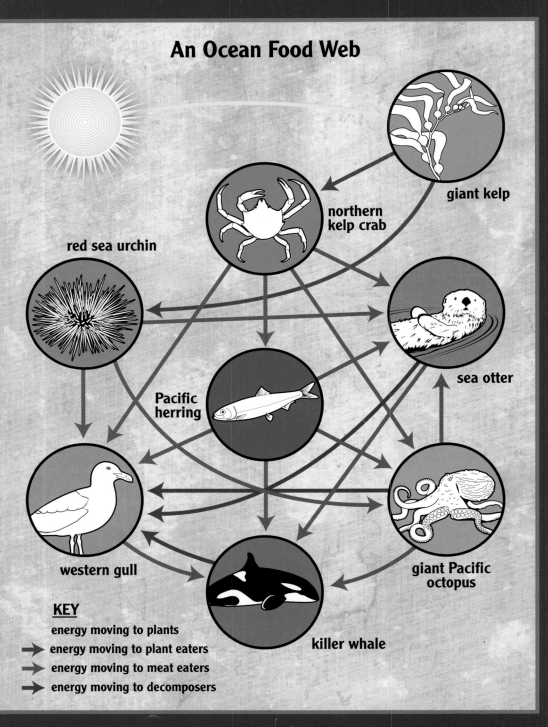

giant kelp

northern kelp crab

red sea urchin

sea otter

Pacific herring

western gull

giant Pacific octopus

killer whale

KEY

energy moving to plants

➤ energy moving to plant eaters

➤ energy moving to meat eaters

➤ energy moving to decomposers

BE A WORD DETECTIVE

Can you find these words as you read about ocean food webs? Be a detective and try to figure out what they mean. You can turn to the glossary on page 46 for help.

algae

bacteria

carnivores

consumers

decay

decomposers

environment

food chain

food web

herbivores

nutrients

omnivores

photosynthesis

plankton

producers

This is how Earth looks from space. The green parts are land. What are the blue areas?

CHAPTER 1
THE OCEAN

From space, our world looks mostly blue. Look at a globe. Most of the globe is blue. Blue means water. We call our planet *Earth*. Maybe we should call it *Ocean*. Almost three-fourths of the world is covered with ocean.

Most water on Earth is ocean water. Ocean water is salty. It is too salty to drink. But it is

Creatures of all sizes live in the ocean. Some are tiny. They are too small to see. Some are very big. Whales live in the ocean. They are the biggest animals on Earth.

Fish swim in the ocean. Worms burrow in the mud of the ocean floor. Clams live in the mud too. Crabs crawl along the bottom. Seabirds fly above the water. Many creatures live along the shore.

A hawksbill turtle eats a jellyfish in the ocean.

The ocean is a very important environment. An environment is the place where any creature lives. The ocean environment includes the air, water, sand or mud, and weather. It includes other plants and animals too.

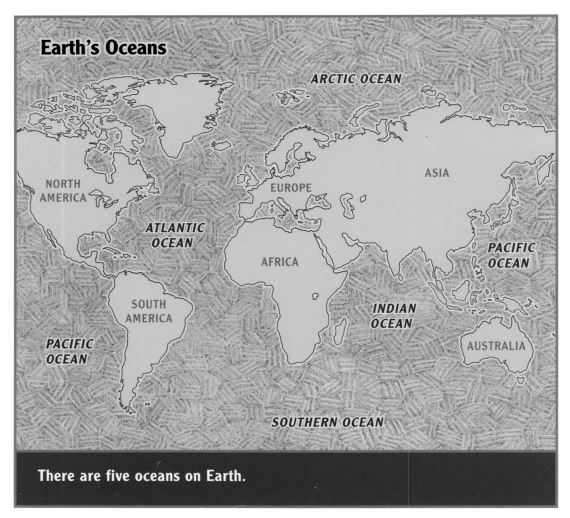

Earth's Oceans

ARCTIC OCEAN

NORTH AMERICA

EUROPE

ASIA

ATLANTIC OCEAN

AFRICA

PACIFIC OCEAN

SOUTH AMERICA

INDIAN OCEAN

PACIFIC OCEAN

AUSTRALIA

SOUTHERN OCEAN

There are five oceans on Earth.

Fin whales and seabirds feed on fish called herring. The herring feed on tiny ocean plants and animals.

Living things in the ocean environment depend on one another. They form a web of life. Some animals eat plants. Other animals are meat eaters. Some creatures feed on dead plants and animals. When plants and animals die, they break down into chemicals (KEH-muh-kuhlz). The chemicals help other plants grow.

Living things get energy from food. Energy moves from one living thing to another. A food chain shows how the energy moves. The energy for life comes from the sun. The sun's energy is stored in plants. Animals eat the plants. They get some of the sun's energy from the plants. The energy moves along the food chain. When one creature eats another, some of the energy is passed on.

Turban snails get energy from food they scrape off kelp.

This harbor seal caught a fish.

There are many food chains in the ocean. Here is one example. A snail eats plants. Then a fish eats the snail. Then a seal eats the fish. When the seal dies, crabs eat its body. Some of the sun's energy goes from the plants to the snail. Then energy is passed to the fish. Then energy goes to the seal. Crabs get energy from the dead seal.

A food web is made of many food chains. Fish eat other things besides snails. They eat clams. They also eat worms and other fish. Seals eat many different kinds of fish. They eat octopuses and squid too. Crabs feed on all kinds of dead animals and plants. Everything each creature eats is part of a food web. A food web shows how all living things in an environment depend on one another for food.

This herring gull has found a dead fish to eat.

Sunlight shines through a giant kelp forest. Kelp and other ocean plants use sunlight to make food. What else do they make?

CHAPTER 2
OCEAN PLANTS

Green plants use sunlight to make food. Living things that make their own food are called producers. Animals use the food plants produce. Plants also make oxygen (AHK-sih-juhn). Oxygen is a gas in the air and water. Animals need oxygen to breathe.

Plants make food and oxygen through photosynthesis (FOH-toh-SIHN-thuh-sihs). Plants need sunlight for photosynthesis. They also need carbon dioxide and water. Carbon dioxide is a gas in the air. It is in the water too. Plants take in carbon dioxide. They take in water. Plants use energy from sunlight to turn water and carbon dioxide into sugar and starch. Sugar and starch are the plants' food. Plants store the food in their bodies.

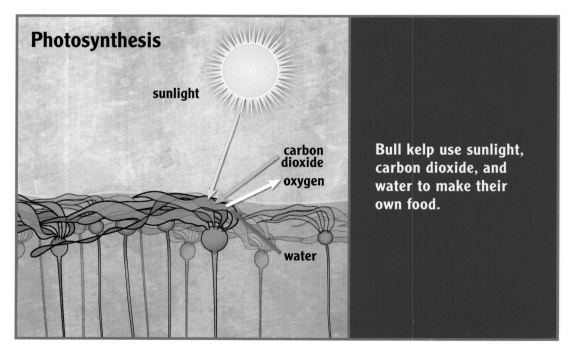

Photosynthesis

sunlight

carbon dioxide

oxygen

water

Bull kelp use sunlight, carbon dioxide, and water to make their own food.

Ocean plants make oxygen that animals breathe. Fish use gills to get oxygen from the water.

Plants also make oxygen as they make food. The oxygen goes into the air and the water. Animals breathe the oxygen. They breathe out carbon dioxide. Plants use the carbon dioxide to make more food.

Water contains chemicals called nutrients (NOO-tree-uhnts). Living things need nutrients to grow. Plants get nutrients when they take in water. The nutrients become part of the plants.

Algae (AL-jee) are plants that float in the water. Most algae are too small to see. But huge numbers of algae grow in the ocean. Algae make the water look green.

Some algae are a kind of plankton. Plankton are living creatures that float and drift in the water. Some plankton are producers. Other plankton are small animals.

Algae grow on a beach in France.

Algae cover rocks along this ocean coast.

Algae are the most important producers on Earth. Algae make most of the oxygen that animals breathe. Ocean animals also eat algae.

Algae need sunlight to grow. Sunlight is brighter near the surface of the ocean. So algae grow only near the surface.

Large algae called seaweeds also live in the ocean. Most seaweeds grow near the shore. Some seaweeds float on the surface of the ocean.

Blue rockfish swim through a giant kelp forest. Giant kelp is a kind of seaweed. It can grow 100 feet tall!

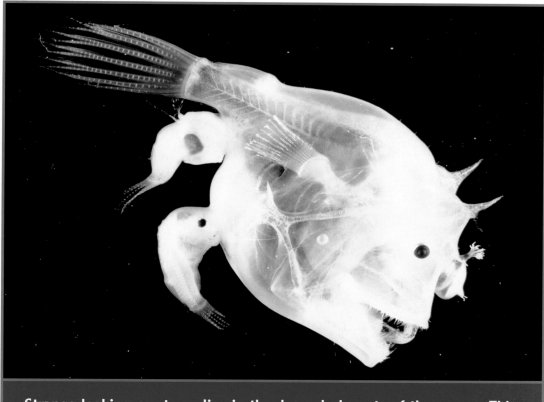

Strange-looking creatures live in the deep, dark parts of the ocean. This deep-sea angler feeds on other fish. Those fish eat food that drifts down from the surface.

No algae grow in the deep parts of the ocean. Light cannot reach there. The deep waters are dark. But deepwater animals need algae too. They need the oxygen algae make. They depend on the animals that eat the algae.

This northern kelp crab lives and feeds on kelp. What other ocean animals eat plants?

CHAPTER 3
OCEAN PLANT EATERS

Living things that eat other living things are consumers. *Consume* means "eat." Animals are consumers.

Animals that eat plants are called herbivores (ER-buh-vorz). The sun's energy is stored in the plants. When an animal eats plants, it gets the sun's energy.

Most ocean herbivores are small. Tiny animal plankton float in the ocean. Many animal plankton feed on algae. Small worms eat algae. So do baby clams and shrimp.

Copepods (KOH-puh-pahdz) are also a kind of animal plankton. They look like tiny shrimp. Copepods eat algae.

This is a copepod. Copepods are very small. They are not much bigger than the periods on this page.

Oysters eat algae too. Oysters take in water. They strain algae out of it. Clams also filter algae from the water.

Snails scrape algae from rocks to eat. Snails also eat kelp. Sea urchins feed on kelp. So do kelp crabs.

This clam is taking in water filled with tiny algae.

Blue tang swim by a coral reef. The fish feed on algae that grow on the reef.

Some larger animals eat algae. Green sea turtles graze on algae. Some fish eat algae too. Blue tang eat algae growing on coral reefs. Corals are tiny ocean animals that build stony homes. Over many years, the corals' homes pile up to make a rocky reef. Many ocean plants and animals live in and around coral reefs.

Octopuses hunt near the ocean floor for other animals to eat. What are animals that eat meat called?

CHAPTER 4
OCEAN MEAT EATERS

Most ocean animals eat meat. Meat-eating animals are called carnivores (KAHR-nuh-vorz). Carnivores catch and eat other animals. Carnivores depend on plants too. Carnivores get energy by eating animals that have eaten plants.

Many ocean animals eat animal plankton. Jellyfish catch plankton in their long, thin tentacles. Sea anemones (uh-NEH-muh-neez) also catch small animals in their tentacles.

A white-spotted rose anemone feeds on a jellyfish.

Ocean fish eat other animals. Sea bass eat worms and crabs. They hunt small fish. Bluefish and tuna are fast swimmers. They catch smaller fish to eat. Some sharks eat bluefish and tuna. Sharks also eat octopuses and other large ocean animals.

A blue shark takes a mouthful of anchovies.

This seal was almost food for a hungry killer whale.

Octopuses are carnivores. They hunt for crabs. Octopuses eat lobsters too.

Whales are meat eaters. Some whales eat animal plankton. Right whales eat copepods. Killer whales hunt for fish. They also attack birds and seals.

Seals and sea otters eat fish. Sea otters also feed on sea urchins and crabs.

Seabirds also feed on fish. Pelicans dive into the water. They catch fish in their beaks. Gulls and terns catch fish too.

A sea otter bites into a crab.

A red and black anemonefish hides in a sea anemone. The fish eats algae and copepods near the anemone.

Some consumers eat both plants and animals. These animals are called omnivores (AHM-nuh-vorz). Damselfish are omnivores. Damselfish eat algae. They also eat animal plankton and small, shrimplike animals.

Some fish gather plankton in their mouths as they swim. These plankton-feeders are omnivores. They gather both plant and animal plankton to eat. Herring and anchovies swim in large groups. These fish swim with their mouths open. They feed on the plankton they catch.

Mole crabs are omnivores. Mole crabs burrow in wet sand. They filter the water in the sand for plankton to eat.

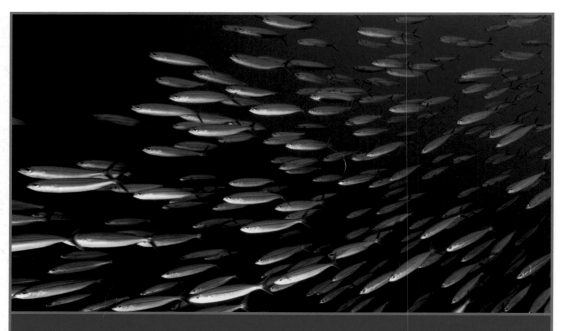

A school of herring zooms through the water.

CHAPTER 5

OCEAN DECOMPOSERS

All living things die. When plants or animals die, they decay. They break down into nutrients. Living things called decomposers help dead things decay. Decomposers feed on

Something has killed a large number of fish in this part of the ocean. Decomposers will break down the bodies into nutrients for algae and other ocean plants.

Decomposers are nature's recyclers. They help break down dead plants and animals. Dead creatures sink to the bottom of the ocean. Decomposers feed on them. The dead plants and animals slowly become part of the mud. Nutrients from them go back into the water. Then other living things can use the nutrients again.

Decomposers are very important. Without them, the ocean would be full of dead plants and animals. Then no new plants could grow. Animals would run out of food.

Some ocean animals are scavengers. They find and eat the bodies of dead animals. Some sharks feed on dead animals floating on the surface of the water. Crabs and lobsters live on the ocean floor. They eat dead animals that sink to the bottom.

This lobster found a meal on the ocean floor.

Sea cucumbers live near the ocean floor. They hold on to rocks or crawl along the sand. Sea cucumbers swallow sand. They eat bits of dead things in the sand.

A sea cucumber uses its sticky tentacles to pick bits of food off a coral reef.

A crab scurries across the body of a dead sea turtle. Crabs and other animals will pick away at the body. Tiny bacteria will break down what is left.

Bacteria (bak-TEER-ee-uh) are the ocean's most important decomposers. Billions of tiny bacteria live in the water. Billions more live in the mud. Bacteria feed on dead creatures in the water and mud. They break down the creatures into nutrients.

A diver swims near a coral reef. Why do people enjoy the ocean?

CHAPTER 6
PEOPLE AND THE OCEAN

The ocean is very important to people. We eat food from the ocean. We travel across the ocean and live by its shores. Ocean algae make

The ocean affects our climate. Ocean water holds heat. The water flows to cooler parts of the world. It carries heat with it. The ocean makes the weather warmer in those places. Cold ocean water flows to other places on Earth. It cools the land there.

The ocean takes in and stores the sun's heat. It carries that heat to other places on Earth.

People build cities near the ocean. These cities have ports. Big ships come into the ports. These ships carry products across the ocean. Ocean ports let people trade with faraway places.

This port is near New York City. The ships carry products across the Atlantic Ocean.

These fishers caught herring. People eat the fish and their eggs. Companies also use herring to make fish oils and animal feed.

People and their activities can harm ocean animals. There are lots of fish in the ocean. People catch fish to eat. Sometimes people catch too many fish from one place. These fish die out. Ocean animals that eat those fish must find other food.

Wastewater pours into the ocean.

People can harm ocean water too. People put fertilizer on lawns or farmland. Fertilizer has nutrients. It helps plants grow. Sewage also has nutrients. Sewage is waste and water carried away in sewers and drains. Rain washes fertilizer and sewage into rivers. The rivers flow into the ocean. The nutrients from the land enter the ocean.

The extra nutrients can make algae grow too fast. That makes the water cloudy. Then underwater plants cannot get enough light. They may die.

Algae use the nutrients. Then the algae die. When they decay, bacteria feed on them. The extra bacteria use up oxygen in the water. Animals in the water may not be able to get enough oxygen to breathe.

These fish died because they could not get enough oxygen from the water. Bacteria used up the oxygen.

The ocean is huge. But it is still harmed if we use it as a place to get rid of waste. Sea life dies if we dump waste in the ocean. People can work to keep fertilizer and sewage out of the ocean. We can also change the way we catch fish so that we don't take too many.

Trash on the ocean's shore can get washed into the water. Picking up the trash helps keep the ocean clean.

Two girls run along an
ocean shore.

People love to visit the ocean. We go to the
beach. We swim and catch fish. But the ocean
is more important than that. It gives us food. It
gives us oxygen. It keeps our climate mild. We
must take good care of the ocean environment.

LEARN MORE ABOUT
OCEANS AND FOOD WEBS

BOOKS

Cerullo, Mary M. *Sea Turtles: Ocean Nomads*. New York: Dutton's Children's Books, 2003. Learn about these ancient and endangered animals.

Johnson, Rebecca L. *A Journey into the Ocean*. Minneapolis: Carolrhoda Books, 2004. Follow a sea turtle's life from the shore into the ocean.

Markle, Sandra. *Octopuses*. Minneapolis: Lerner Publications Company, 2007. Read about these fascinating creatures of the sea.

Taylor, Leighton. *Anemone Fish*. Lerner Publications Company, 2007. Discover what life is like for clownfish, fish that make their homes in sea anemones.

Taylor, Leighton. *Great White Sharks*. Lerner Publications Company, 2006. Find out about these fierce ocean hunters.

Woodward, John. *Oceans Atlas*. New York: DK Children, 2007. This is an ocean-by-ocean survey of the world.

WEBSITES

Monterey Bay Aquarium: Kid's Corner
http://www.mbayaq.org/lc/
Check out games, music, video clips of ocean animals in action, and much more.

Ocean Living for Kids
http://nationalzoo.si.edu/Animals/OceanLiving/ForKids
Get the facts on seals and sea lions from the Smithsonian National Zoological Park website.

GLOSSARY

algae (AL-jee): water plants that use sunlight to make food. Some algae are tiny. Other algae, such as seaweeds, are large.

bacteria (bak-TEER-ee-uh): tiny living things made of just one cell. Bacteria can be seen only under a microscope.

carnivores (KAHR-nuh-vorz): animals that eat meat

consumers: living things that eat other living things. Animals are consumers.

decay: to break down

decomposers: living things that feed on dead plants and animals and break them down into nutrients

environment: a place where a creature lives. An ocean environment includes the air, water, sand or mud, weather, plants, and animals in a place.

food chain: the way energy moves from the sun to a plant, then to a plant eater, then to a meat eater, and finally to a decomposer

food web: many food chains connected together. A food web shows how all living things in a place need each other for food.

herbivores (ER-buh-vorz): animals that eat plants

nutrients (NOO-tree-uhnts): chemicals that living things need in order to grow

omnivores (AHM-nuh-vorz): animals that eat both plants and animals

photosynthesis (FOH-toh-SIHN-thuh-sihs): the way green plants use energy from sunlight to make their own food from carbon dioxide and water

plankton: small plants and animals that float in the ocean

producers: living things that make their own food. Plants are producers.

scavengers: animals that eat dead plants and animals

INDEX